How to Draw the Life and Times of
James K. Polk

Melody S. Mis

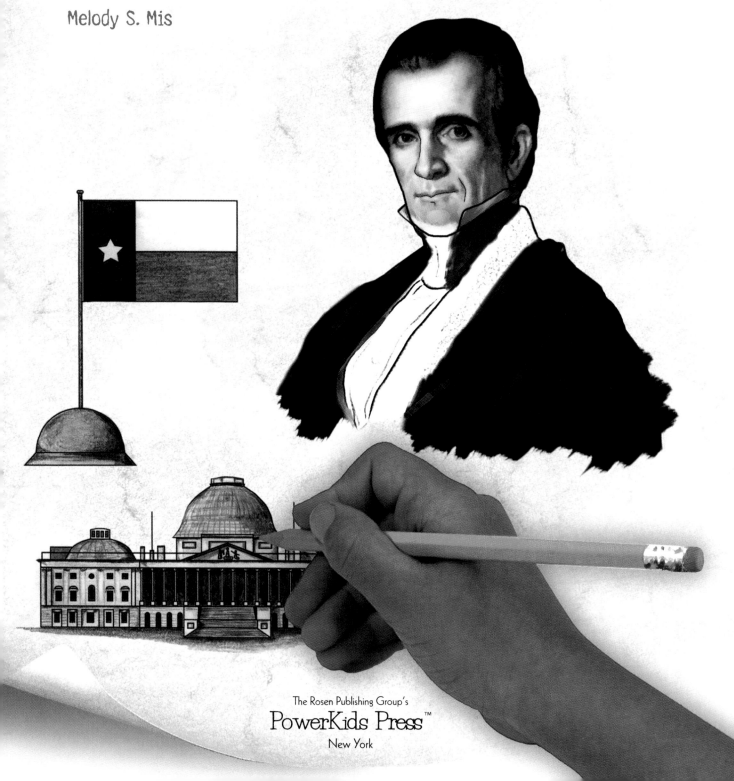

The Rosen Publishing Group's
PowerKids Press™
New York

To clowns everywhere, for bringing joy and laughter to others

Published in 2006 by The Rosen Publishing Group, Inc.
29 East 21st Street, New York, NY 10010

First Edition

Editor: Jennifer Way
Layout Design: Ginny Chu

Illustrations: All illustrations by Holly Cefrey.
Photo Credits: p. 4 Courtesy of the Naval Historical Center; p. 7 © Bettmann/Corbis; pp. 8 (left), 12 James K. Polk Memorial Association, Columbia, Tennessee; p. 9 Michael Reed; p. 10 Courtesy of the North Carolina State Archives; pp. 14, 28 Library of Congress Prints and Photographs Division; p. 16 From the Collection of Studebaker National Museum, South Bend, Indiana; p. 18 Courtesy of the Texas State Library and Archives Commission; p. 20 The Mariners' Museum, Newport News, VA; p. 22 National Postal Museum, Smithsonian Institution; p. 24 © Carl & Ann Purcell/Corbis; p. 26 Courtesy of the Women's Rights National Historical Park.

Library of Congress Cataloging-in-Publication Data

Mis, Melody S.
How to draw the life and times of James K. Polk / Melody S. Mis.— 1st ed.
    p. cm. — (A kid's guide to drawing the presidents of the United States of America)
Includes bibliographical references and index.
ISBN 1-4042-2988-4 (lib. bdg.)
1. Polk, James K. (James Knox), 1795–1849—Juvenile literature. 2. Presidents—United States—Biography—Juvenile literature. 3. Drawing—Technique—Juvenile literature. I. Title. II. Series.
E417.M57 2006
973.6'1'092—dc22
                                    2004021844

Manufactured in the United States of America

Contents

James K. Polk

James Knox Polk was born on November 2, 1795, in Mecklenburg County near Charlotte, North Carolina. He was the first of 10 children born to Samuel and Jane Polk. When James was 11 years old, his family moved to Duck River Valley, Tennessee.

Polk was educated at home until he was 17. In 1815, he entered the University of North Carolina in Chapel Hill. Polk graduated near the top of his class and went to Nashville, Tennessee, to study law. In 1819, Polk got a job as clerk for the Tennessee Senate, which met in Murfreesboro. During this time Polk met Sarah Childress, whom he married in 1824.

In 1823, Polk had been elected to the Tennessee House of Representatives. In 1825, Polk was elected to the U.S. House of Representatives. He served seven two-year terms. From 1835 to 1839, Polk served as Speaker of the House of Representatives. The Speaker runs the meetings of the U.S. House of Representatives.

In 1839, Polk was elected governor of Tennessee. After Polk lost his reelection bid in 1844, he became the Democrats' presidential nominee. The Democrats chose Polk because he wanted to expand U.S. territory.

Polk's campaign slogan of "Fifty-four Forty or Fight" showed his aim to gain the Oregon Territory, even if it meant war with Britain, which controlled the territory. The slogan referred to the map latitude of the northern border the United States wanted to establish with Canada. Polk had to compromise, however, and the border was set at 49° latitude, instead of 54° 40' latitude. Polk was elected as the nation's eleventh president.

You will need the following supplies to draw the life and times of James K. Polk:

✓ A sketch pad   ✓ An eraser   ✓ A pencil   ✓ A ruler

These are some of the shapes and drawing terms you need to know:

Horizontal Line	——		Squiggly Line	〰
Oval	⬭		Trapezoid	⏢
Rectangle	▭		Triangle	△
Shading	▰		Vertical Line	│
Slanted Line	╱		Wavy Line	∿

The Manifest Destiny President

James Polk is known as the Manifest Destiny president, because he was responsible for one of the largest growths of U.S. territory. "Manifest Destiny" was the term for the nineteenth-century idea that it was the United States' purpose to expand across the North American continent from the Atlantic Ocean to the Pacific Ocean. Polk added more territory to the United States than did any other president.

Polk set out to accomplish many goals during his presidency, which lasted from 1845 to 1849. Texas was admitted as the twenty-eighth state in 1845. In 1846, Polk worked out a treaty with Great Britain, which established the border between the United States and Canada in the West. Two years later Polk purchased California from Mexico.

Polk is often praised as one of the nation's hardest-working presidents. During his four years as president, Polk spent a total of six weeks away from his office. It is because of Polk's hard work that he could achieve the goals that he set for his term of office.

Polk was inaugurated, or sworn into office, on March 4, 1845. He took this vow before a crowd in front of the Capitol in Washington, D.C. This print of the inauguration originally appeared in the *Illustrated London News* in 1845.

Polk's Tennessee

Tennessee

Map of the United States of America

James Polk lived at the Polk Home from 1818, when he began his law career, until he married in 1824.

James Polk lived most of his life in Tennessee, but only one of his homes still exists. It is the Polk Home in Columbia, Tennessee. The Polk Home is one of the best examples of Federal-style architecture in Tennessee. Federal-style architecture features brick faces and a front door topped with a decorative half-circle window called a fanlight. Polk's father, Samuel, built the home in 1816. James visited the family home during his vacations from the University of North Carolina. James lived in this home from 1818, when he moved to Columbia to start a law practice, until he married Sarah Childress in 1824.

Polk's tomb is now on the grounds of the Tennessee state capitol in Nashville.

The home, which is open to the public, displays furniture, White House china, and gifts that Polk received during his presidency. On the grounds of the home there is a fountain that was taken from James and Sarah's home in Nashville, called Polk Place. The home was torn down in 1901.

When Polk died in 1849, he was buried in the garden at Polk Place in Nashville. Sarah died in 1891. In 1893, the state of Tennessee honored Polk by moving him and Sarah to Capitol Hill, where they were buried near the front entrance of the Tennessee capitol building. The tomb was created by William Strickland, who was a famous nineteenth-century architect.

James K. Polk's Birthplace

James Polk was born to Samuel and Jane Polk on November 2, 1795. His birthplace was a log cabin located near Little Sugar Creek in Mecklenburg County, North Carolina. The

cabin was part of a 250-acre (100 ha) farm that was a gift to Samuel from his father, Ezekial. James' birthplace was actually two cabins that may have had a covered walkway between them. The original log cabins and farm buildings were torn down in 1920. A farm similar to that owned by the Polks was rebuilt on the property in 1967 to show what the original buildings looked like.

The main part of the cabin has a fireplace and four rooms, two upstairs and two downstairs. The furniture in the cabin is from the late eighteenth century. Other buildings on the farm include a kitchen and a small barn. Today Polk's birthplace is a museum that is open to the public.

1

Begin James Polk's birthplace by drawing two shapes.

2

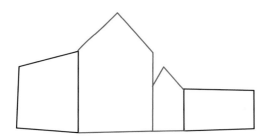

Draw the sides of the buildings using the peaked shapes.

3

Add the buildings' roofs. Draw nine rectangles on the buildings. Some are doors and some are windows.

4

Draw lines across the cabins. These are the logs. Erase any lines that go through the windows or doorways. Add horizontal and vertical lines to the windows to make panes. Add a vertical line inside the right door on the building on the left.

5

Draw more logs on the buildings. Add a chimney to each building.

6

Finish with shading. This will give the rough look of the logs and the smooth look of the roofs. Great job!

Meet Sarah Childress Polk

Sarah Childress was born on September 4, 1803, on a plantation near Murfreesboro, Tennessee. She was the third of six children born to Joel and Elizabeth Childress. Sarah's father was a wealthy farmer and businessman. In 1817, he sent Sarah and her sister, Susan, to the Moravian Female Academy  in Salem, North Carolina. When Joel Childress died in 1819, the girls left school to help their mother at home.

Around 1822, Sarah met James Polk in Murfreesboro. She was 20 years old and Polk was 28 years old when they married on January 1, 1824. When Polk became president in 1845, Sarah acted as his secretary. Sarah was deeply religious and did not allow dancing or card playing in the White House.

After James died Sarah continued to live at Polk Place in Nashville, Tennessee, until she died on August 14, 1891. She is buried alongside her husband in the tomb on Capitol Hill in Nashville.

1 Begin by drawing a slanted vertical line. Then draw a slanted horizontal line across the vertical line. These will be the guides to draw the shoulders. Draw an oval at the top of it.

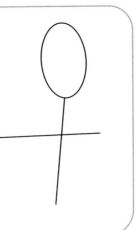

2 Draw the eyes, nose, and mouth guides in the oval as shown.

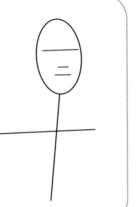

3 Draw the basic body shape as shown. Draw almond-shaped ovals for the eyes.

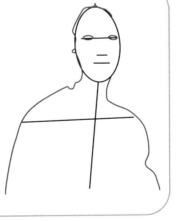

4 Erase the body guidelines. Draw her eyebrows, nose, and mouth as shown. Erase the rest of the head oval, near the hairline. Erase the eye guidelines.

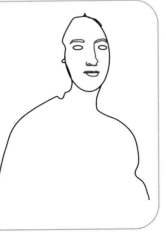

5 Erase the nose and mouth guides. Draw circles in the eyes and eyelids as shown. Add the outline of her hair. Draw curls on the side of her head.

6 Draw pupils in the eyes. Draw the rest of her hair. Draw her clothing as shown.

7 Finish with detailed shading. Her dress is very dark. Her hair is dark. You can use the side of your pencil tip to shade in the background.

The House of Representatives

James Polk served in the U.S. House of Representatives from 1825 to 1839. He served as Speaker of the House of Representatives from 1835 to 1839. The U.S. House of Representatives is part of the legislative branch of the U.S. government. When Polk served in the House of Representatives, he fought to lower peoples' taxes and to lower taxes on goods from foreign countries.

The U.S. House of Representatives is located on the second floor of the Capitol in Washington, D.C. The Capitol, shown above, was built in 1793. It has burned several times and been repaired and has been expanded into the beautiful neoclassical building we see today. Neoclassical architecture features columns and domes like those found on ancient Greek and Roman temples. Inside the Capitol there are five floors, 540 rooms, and three public areas, including the Rotunda, which is used for special events.

1

Use a ruler to draw a large horizontal rectangle. This will be the front of the building. Draw a guideline down the center of it.

2

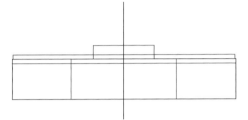

Draw a small rectangle on top of the first rectangle. Draw the long, thin shape across the top as shown. Draw the horizontal and vertical lines on the front of the building.

3

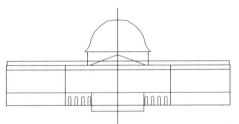

Draw the dome. Add two lines to make the pointed roof. Draw a horizontal line across the front of the building. Draw a rectangle under this line. Draw eight arch shapes.

4

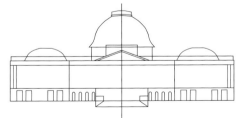

Add a dome on each side. Draw the shapes on the roof and the center dome. Draw doors along the front. Begin to draw the stairs. Begin to draw the columns. Erase extra lines.

5

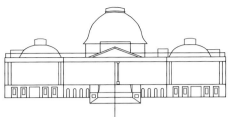

Draw more columns. Add to the roof and the domes as shown. Add lines to the front as shown. Draw lines on the stairs and two rectangles. Erase part of the center guideline.

6

Erase the rest of the center guide. Add more columns. Draw shapes on the domes. Add two horizontal lines on each side of the building. Add two rectangles to the row of doors.

7

Draw the windows. Draw the shapes on the roof. Draw the figures in the triangular part of the roof. Add tiny triangles on each side of the building near the roof.

8

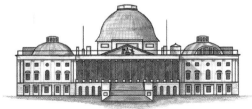

Erase the guidelines. Finish with shading. The space between the columns is very dark. The windows and doors are very dark, too. Good job!

The Oregon Trail

In the 1830s, the first settlers began to travel on the Oregon Trail to the Oregon Territory in what is now the northwest of the United States. After James Polk became president in 1845, he fulfilled his  campaign promise of acquiring this territory from Great Britain in 1846. The territory included the present states of Washington, Oregon, and Idaho, plus part of Montana and Wyoming. This was one of the reasons Polk was known as the Manifest Destiny president.

The Oregon Trail was 2,000 miles (3,219 km) long and stretched from Missouri to Oregon. Thousands of pioneers used the trail to move west, seeking the promise of Oregon's huge forests and free land. The pioneers traveled in wagons, such as the one shown above, that were made of wood and covered with a waterproof cloth hood. The hood protected the pioneers' supplies. There was little room inside the wagons, so most pioneers walked the Oregon Trail.

1

Begin by drawing the body of the wagon as shown. It has straight lines and curvy lines.

2

Draw the hood of the wagon as shown. The top is a straight line that you will erase later. Draw the curvy line underneath the body.

3

Erase extra lines. Draw a wavy line across the top of the hood. Add the opening at the front. Draw two ovals for wheels.

4

Erase extra lines. Draw the lines on the wagon and inside the cover. Add another wheel. Draw curvy lines on the side of the wheels.

5

Erase extra lines. Add more curves in the wheels. Draw the folds on the cover. Draw the lines on the front of the wagon.

6

Add more lines to the side of the wagon body. Draw ropes on the flaps of the cover. Draw the axles between the wheels as shown.

7

Draw the spokes on the wheels. Draw the shape above the front axle. Draw the shape in the back of the wagon body as shown.

8

Erase the parts of the axles that go through the spokes. Finish with detailed shading. The wheels and axles are very dark. Great work!

The Annexation of Texas

On February 28, 1845, just a few days before Polk took office as president, the U.S. Congress offered to annex Texas, with the aim of making it a state. Texas had been a republic since 1836, when it had gained independence from Mexico in the Texas Revolution. The Lone Star flag was adopted as the flag of the Republic of Texas in 1839 and is still in use.

A debate began surrounding the annexation of Texas. Some people feared that it would be admitted as a state where slavery would be allowed. The northern states, where slavery was not allowed, did not want to admit another slave state. The southern states, where slavery was permitted, did. The majority of Americans favored the annexation of Texas because it expanded the nation's territory. Polk achieved one of his campaign goals when Texas became the twenty-eighth state on December 29, 1845.

1

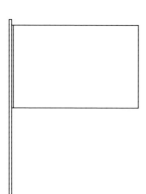

Use your ruler to draw a large horizontal rectangle. This will be the flag. Draw the pole next to it. Draw tiny lines from the flag to the pole.

3

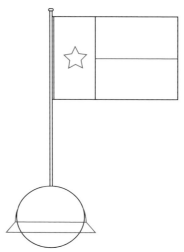

Draw the trapezoid on the oval. This will become the base of the flagpole. Draw small curved lines to connect the trapezoid to the oval. Draw a star in the left section of the flag. Draw a horizontal line in the flag.

2

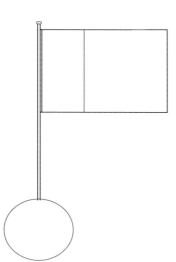

Add a small oval to the top of the post. Draw the large oval at the end of the post. Draw a vertical line in the flag. It is not in the middle. It is over to the left.

4

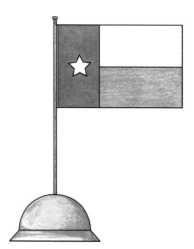

Erase extra lines. Finish with shading. The rectangle with the lone star is the darkest. Texas's nickname is the "Lone Star State." "Lone" means all by itself.

The Mexican War

When Texas declared its independence from Mexico, it set its border at the Rio Grande. Mexico placed the border at the Nueces River, which was 150 miles (241 km) north  of the Rio Grande. Neither side wanted to compromise on where the border would be.

When Texas became a state in 1845, Polk ordered troops sent there to protect its border with Mexico. When Mexican soldiers attacked the American troops, Polk declared war on Mexico on May 13, 1846. In addition to American troops fighting along the Texas border, the navy was sent to the Gulf of Mexico, where the USS *Mississippi*, shown above, helped in the war.

Mexico was defeated in 1848, and the war ended with the Treaty of Guadalupe Hidalgo. This treaty established the Rio Grande as Texas's southern border. Polk was praised for winning the war, because of the sizable territory the United States gained.

1

You will draw the USS *Mississippi*. Begin by drawing the body of the boat. Draw a squiggly line for the water.

2

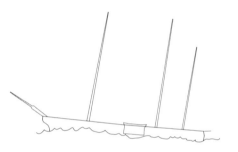

Draw the three masts. Add the pole at the front of the boat and the short line at the back. Draw the shape on the body of the boat. The paddle wheel will go behind it.

3

Erase extra lines. Draw the anchor on the front of the boat. Add the steam pipe and the paddle wheel. Draw the sail as shown. Draw the lines on the masts. These are what stretch the sails.

4

Draw the line on the anchor. Draw more sails. Add flags to the masts. Add lines to the masts, the pole on the back of the boat, and the paddle wheel. Draw two lifeboats near the back of the boat. Add more water lines.

5

Erase extra lines. Add three more sails. Add lines on the side of the boat and the paddle wheel. Add a shape on the flag. Add lines to the lifeboats. Draw more squiggly lines in the water.

6

Erase extra lines. Finish with shading. The sails have lines on them that you can draw to show the folds in the cloth. The water has many waves and looks choppy. Great job!

The First U.S. Postage Stamp

Before Polk became president in 1845, postage rates were high. This was because they were based on the number of sheets of paper to be mailed instead of the weight of the letter. In 1845, a law established standard postage rates. However, there were still no prepaid stamps available to attach to mail, as we have today.

In 1847, Polk signed the Post Office Act, which gave the U.S. Post Office the right to issue the first prepaid U.S. postage stamps. Stamps with the prepaid postage on them made it easier and faster to process mail.

The postmaster general selected the color of the new stamps and the subjects that would be printed on them. The five-cent stamp was brown and had a picture of Benjamin Franklin on it. The black ten-cent stamp featured a picture of George Washington.

1

You will be drawing a Benjamin Franklin stamp. Begin by drawing a large rectangle. Draw two ovals, one inside of the other.

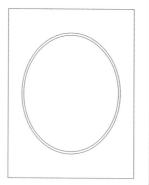

2

Draw a second rectangle inside of the first one. Draw a large oval for the head. Draw a curved line next to it for the side of the head. Draw a slanted oval for the ear.

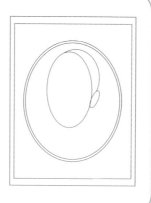

3

Draw guidelines for Franklin's eyes, nose, and mouth. Draw a curved line for his cheek and jaw. Write the letters *U* and *S* as shown. Write the number 5 in both lower corners.

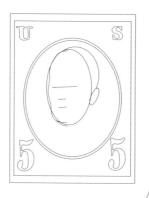

4

Write "POST OFFICE" above the oval. Draw almond shapes for the eyes. Add the nose and mouth. Use wavy lines to make Franklin's hair and collar.

5

Erase the head guidelines. Draw the eyebrows. Add lines to Franklin's face and hair. Add lines to his ear. Write "FIVE CENTS" along the bottom of the oval.

6

Erase extra lines on the head, ear, and eyes. Draw the rest of Franklin's clothing. Finish his hair with wavy lines. Add lines around his eyes and on his forehead. Draw pupils in his eyes.

7

Finish with shading. To shade it like the stamp, shade with lines. There are dark and light lines. There are dark shadows behind the letters and numbers. Very good!

The California Gold Rush

On January 24, 1848, gold was discovered at Sutter's Mill, on the American River in northern California. John Sutter wanted to keep the discovery a secret, but the news soon spread. This

news meant that the territory Polk had recently gained with the Treaty of Guadalupe Hidalgo was even more valuable than was originally believed.

Stories about California gold were carried in newspapers. In December 1848, Polk told the nation that these stories were true. He had seen the gold firsthand when a piece was brought to Washington, D.C. After Polk's announcement many people went west to take part in the California gold rush.

These gold seekers, called prospectors, purchased tools such as picks and shovels, like those shown above, so they could get the gold out of the riverbeds. Some prospectors became rich, but most were not so lucky.

1

You will be drawing a pick and a shovel, which were used as mining tools during the gold rush. Begin by drawing the guidelines for the tools. One is a *T*. It will be the pick. The other is a straight line. Notice how the lines cross to form an *X*.

2

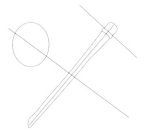

Draw the large oval as shown. This will become the shovel. Use the guideline to draw a handle on the pick.

3

Erase the guideline for the pick's handle. Draw the head of the pick. Draw the handle of the shovel as shown.

4

Erase the remaining guide for the pick and the straight shovel guideline. Draw the shape of the shovel head. Erase the extra lines where the pick and the shovel cross. Draw two lines on the pick. Draw a small line at the end of the shovel handle. Add a circle and a curved line to the shovel handle.

5

Erase extra lines. Finish with shading. The shovel and pick are very dark. The handles are lighter. Great work!

The Seneca Falls Convention

In Polk's first speech to the nation when he took office in 1845, he noted that the U.S. Constitution gave all American citizens equal rights. At this time

women were beginning their struggle to get equal rights. On July 19, 1848, the Seneca Falls Convention was held. It was the first women's rights convention in the United States. It was held at the Wesleyan Methodist Church, shown above.

One of the organizers of the convention was Elizabeth Cady Stanton. She wrote the Declaration of Sentiments, which explained the rights she believed women should have. This included the right of women to vote. Although Polk did not support suffrage for women, the issue became more important as the country grew. It is because of the women's rights movement that women today have many of the same rights as men. The Wesleyan Methodist church is now a national historic park and is open to the public.

1

You will be drawing the Wesleyan Methodist Church, where the Seneca Falls Convention was held. Begin by using a ruler to draw the shape as shown. Make the top line of the shape longer on the left side.

2

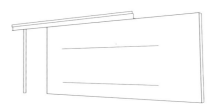

Add the long straight lines inside the wall and on the right side of the wall. The horizontal lines on the wall will be guidelines for the windows. Draw the pole that will hold up the roof. Add the front of the roof.

3

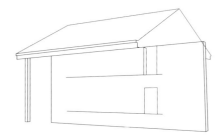

Draw the roof. Begin to draw the windows. The top window has a narrow side. Add another line to the roof-support pole.

4

Erase extra lines, including the top of the upper window. Draw the diagonal line inside the window. Add four more windows. Draw the diagonal lines near the pole. Add the shape on top of the roof as shown. Add a vertical line to the right side wall.

5

Erase the window guidelines. Draw sides to the other five windows. Add a diagonal line in the upper right window. Add a post on the back right side of the chapel. Draw a long straight line on the rooftop. Draw the rain gutter on the left pole.

6

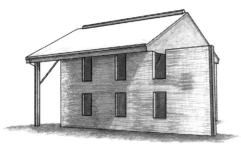

Finish with detailed shading. The windows are very dark. The sides of the windows are light. Shade the walls with light and dark lines. This will make it look like it is made of bricks. You can shade the ground, too. Well done!

Polk's Legacy

James Polk was exhausted when he left office in 1849 and returned to Nashville. Three months after his return, Polk died, possibly of cholera, at age 53 on June 15, 1849.

During Polk's term, four states were admitted to the Union, increasing the nation's territory by 1.2 million square miles (3.1 million sq km). Under Polk the Department of Interior was established. This department works with Native Americans, manages land and water resources, and protects America's national parks.

Some people think that Polk spent too much time on westward expansion. This expansion was often accomplished at the expense of the Native Americans, who were forced off their lands as people moved west.

Although there were complaints about Polk's presidency, historians rank him as one of the nation's top presidents. He earned this ranking because of the number of goals he accomplished in his presidency.

1

Begin by drawing a large oval. Draw a vertical line for the body. Draw an oval for the head. Draw an oval for the ear. Draw a curved line for the side of the head. Add guidelines for the eyes, nose, and mouth.

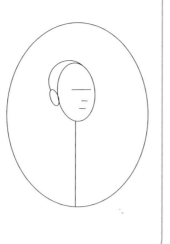

2

Draw almond-shaped ovals for the eyes. Draw the nose and mouth as shown. Draw Polk's cheek and jaw. Draw his neck and body outline.

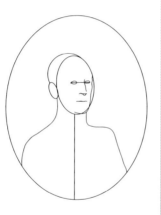

3

Erase the body guideline. Erase part of the head oval and the guidelines for the eyes, nose, and mouth. Draw circles in the eyes. Add an ear. Draw the eyebrows and lines around the mouth. Draw his collar.

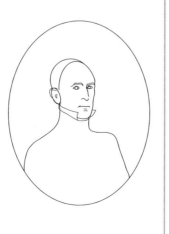

4

Erase extra lines. Draw detail lines around the eyes. Draw his hair. Erase the ear guide. Draw his tie and one side of his jacket collar.

5

Erase the remaining head guidelines and the body lines that cross over the collar. Draw the lines on the face. Add lines in the hair. Draw the rest of his clothing.

6

Erase extra lines. Finish with shading. Parts of his jacket and tie are very dark. His eyes are dark. His hair is very light. Well done!

Timeline

1795 James K. Polk is born in North Carolina.

1815 Polk enters the University of North Carolina.

1818 Polk graduates from the university and begins to study law.

1819–1823 Polk serves as clerk of the Tennessee senate.

1820 Polk opens a law office in Columbia, Tennessee.

1823 Polk is elected to the Tennessee House of Representatives.

1824 Polk marries Sarah Childress.

1825–1839 Polk serves in the U.S. House of Representatives.

1835–1839 Polk is Speaker of the House of Representatives.

1839–1841 Polk serves as governor of Tennessee.

1844 Polk is elected president of the United States.

1845 Texas is annexed to the United States.

Florida is admitted as the twenty-seventh state.

Texas is admitted as the twenty-eighth state.

1846 The United States declares war on Mexico.

Iowa is admitted as the twenty-ninth state.

Wisconsin is admitted as the thirtieth state.

1848 The Treaty of Guadalupe Hidalgo is signed, which ends the Mexican War.

1849 Polk's term as president ends.

Polk dies three months after he returns home to Nashville, Tennessee.

Glossary

annex (A-neks) To take over or to add to.

architecture (AR-kih-tek-cher) The art of creating and making buildings.

cholera (KAH-luh-rah) A painful illness of the stomach that causes pain and throwing up.

compromise (KOM-pruh-myz) To give up something, to reach an agreement.

Congress (KON-gris) The part of the government that makes laws.

declared (dih-KLAYRD) Announced officially.

defeated (dih-FEET-ed) Beaten, conquered.

Democrats (DEH-muh-krats) Members of the Democratic political party.

expand (ek-SPAND) To spread out, or to grow larger.

foreign (FOR-in) From another country or place.

latitude (LA-tih-tood) The distance north or south of the equator, measured by degrees.

legislative (LEH-jis-lay-tiv) Having to do with the branch of government that makes laws and collects taxes.

nominee (nah-mih-NEE) The person who is selected to do a certain job.

plantation (plan-TAY-shun) A very large farm where crops like tobacco and cotton are grown.

representatives (reh-prih-ZEN-tuh-tivs) People who are elected to speak for others.

republic (ree-PUB-lik) A form of government in which the authority belongs to the people.

resources (REE-sors-ez) Things that occur in nature and that can be used or sold, such as gold, coal, or wool.

revolution (reh-vuh-LOO-shun) A complete change in government.

rotunda (roh-TUN-dah) A round building, generally covered by a dome.

sentiments (SEN-tuh-ments) Feelings.

suffrage (SUH-frij) The right of voting.

tomb (TOOM) A place where a dead person is buried.

Index

Web Sites

Due to the changing nature of Internet links, PowerKids Press has developed an online list of Web sites related to the subject of this book. This site is updated regularly. Please use this link to access the list:
www.powerkidslinks.com/kgdpusa/polk/